Introduction

For years, I have been dissatisfied with the standard examinations of conscience which, intending to help people prepare for the sacrament of Reconciliation, provide lists of possible sins. I already know which of those sins I have committed, and the laundry list does not help me dig deeper or more widely. As well, the standard catalogues rarely probe the various milieus of my life – home, work, prayer and engagement with society.

Throughout Pope Francis' pontificate, he has repeatedly asked questions that explore the spiritual state of one's soul. I have fruitfully used the section "Our Daily Love" from the Pope's letter *Amoris Laetitia* (The Joy of Love) to aid my preparation for Reconciliation. In fact, in many of his talks and writings, the Pope has offered practical advice for living a better life. Even more than his predecessors, Pope Francis is a spiritual guide for the ordinary Catholic in the pew. His gift to us is a practical attention to the attitudes and decisions of daily life. He also challenges us to overcome our complacency in the face of social injustice and environmental devastation.

Eventually, I decided to bring together some of his pointed analyses to provide a more thorough approach to the examination of conscience. This little book is the fruit of my research and reflection.

The first thing one might note is that while the book is short, its list of potential faults is long. One might stagger under the weight of knowing all that one does wrong or could be doing better. Laying on heavy burdens is not my intention.

Instead, I propose that these reflections be used as part of a regular meditation on the state of one's life. St. Ignatius of Loyola urged that we conduct a brief examination of ourselves every night. That is a sound practice. But if you see it as too onerous, instead take this book and consider a couple of different meditations two or three times a week. Find a quiet spot where you won't be disturbed, and ask the Lord to be with you during your time of examination. If you wish, enjoy a cup of tea or coffee during the 10 or 20 minutes you spend in reflection. Read the Scripture quote, the quote from Pope Francis and the reflection questions several times. Ask yourself whether the meditation calls you to change some aspect of your life. If it does, resolve how you will do this and commit to take the matter to a priest in Reconciliation.

Be slow to judge yourself. With each meditation, take note of your feelings and insights, but do not condemn yourself for your failures. Give your thoughts and emotions time to gel. It is difficult to discover, let alone admit, one's faults. Because you cannot do all that is good and holy, the most basic discernment is whether you fulfill your unique personal responsibilities. To what is God calling you? How have you responded? Which meditations in this book are relevant to that call and which are not?

Most of us have responsibilities in all four milieus on which this book touches – prayer, family, work and society. In particular, all of us have a responsibility to bring the gospel to bear on society by performing works of mercy and working for social justice. It is that area of life which is most often neglected, either through complacency or through a tone-deafness to the Bible's insistent call to build a more just and peaceful world. We should not ignore our complicity in structures which produce environmental devastation, an idolatry of consumer goods, and a vast inequality between the rich and poor.

Pope Francis says that Jesus "wants us to be saints and not to settle for a bland and mediocre existence." (*Gaudete et Exsultate* [Rejoice and Be Glad], 1) Each person has a unique vocation, one which stands in contrast with the many dehumanizing practices of contemporary life. To follow Jesus is to strive to become a saint. May this little book help you grow in holiness and contribute to the renewal of our society.

Glen Argan

Glen Argan has spent more than 35 years writing and editing in Canada's Catholic press and has two graduate degrees in theology.

MY LIFE OF PRAYER

God's mission for me

It was you who formed my inward parts; you knit me together in my mother's womb. I praise you, for I am fearfully and wonderfully made. (Psalm 139.13-14)

You too need to see the entirety of your life as a mission. Try to do so by listening to God in prayer and recognizing the signs that he gives you. Always ask the Spirit what Jesus expects from you at every moment of your life and in every decision you must make, so as to discern its place in the mission you have received. (*Gaudete et Exsultate*, 23)

- **Do I see myself as playing a role in the unfolding of God's plan for humanity?**
- **How do I discern God's will for my life?**
- **Do I value my own desires for wealth, public acclaim and personal comfort more than I value carrying out my God-given mission?**

Dialogue with God

Come away to a deserted place all by yourselves and rest a while. (Mark 6.31)

We are overwhelmed by words, by superficial pleasures and by an increasing din, filled not by joy but rather by the discontent of those whose lives have lost meaning. How can we fail to realize the need to stop this rat race and to recover the personal space needed to carry on a heartfelt dialogue with God? Finding that space may prove painful but it is always fruitful. (*Gaudete et Exsultate*, 29)

- **Do I attend daily to my relationship with God?**
- **Do I withdraw regularly from life's busy-ness to enter into a heartfelt dialogue with God?**
- **How have I tried to reduce the amount of time and energy I give to "superficial pleasures"?**

Harmony with nature

From your lofty abode you water the mountains; the earth is satisfied with the fruit of your work. (Psalm 104.13)

Many people today sense a profound imbalance which drives them to frenetic activity and makes them feel busy, in a constant hurry which in turn leads them to ride roughshod over everything around them. This too affects how they treat the environment. An integral ecology includes taking time to recover a serene harmony with creation, reflecting on our lifestyle and our ideals, and contemplating the Creator who lives among us and surrounds us. (*Laudato Si'*, 225)

- **Do I take time to contemplate the awesome beauty and order of nature?**
- **Does my prayer include times of silent meditation in which I am open to the gentle presence of the Creator?**
- **Do I ever go for a walk or sit outside with a friend, casually discussing those things which are most important to us?**

Spiritual poverty

The only thing that counts is faith working through love. (Galatians 5.6)

Once we believe that everything depends on human effort as channelled by ecclesial rules and structures, we unconsciously complicate the Gospel and become enslaved to a blueprint that leaves few openings for the working of grace. (*Gaudete et Exsultate*, 59)

- **Am I afraid to rely upon the Holy Spirit and instead seek safety in a bureaucratic or legalistic mentality?**
- **How do I react when I receive no guidance from human authorities and their rules?**
- **Do I see myself as spiritually poor and wholly dependent on God's grace?**

Lost love

I have this against you, that you have abandoned the love you had at first. (Revelation 2.4)

There is also a "spiritual Alzheimer's disease." It consists in losing the memory of our personal "salvation history," our past history with the Lord and our "first love" (Revelation 2.4). It involves a progressive decline in the spiritual faculties which in the long or short run greatly handicaps a person by making him incapable of doing anything on his own, living in a state of absolute dependence on his often imaginary perceptions. (*Pope Francis' 2014 Christmas Greetings to the Roman Curia*)

- I remember and treasure the moments when God touched my life. Have I allowed the passage of time to let my heart grow cold to God?

- Have I lost my sense of the eternal value of each moment?

- Does my "forgetfulness" of God lead me to see my plans and actions solely in practical terms?

Hidden pain

Blessed are those who mourn, for they will be comforted. (Matthew 5.7)

The world has no desire to mourn; it would rather disregard painful situations, cover them up or hide them. Much energy is expended on fleeing from situations of suffering in the belief that reality can be concealed. But the cross can never be absent. (*Gaudete et Exsultate,* 75)

- **Do I try to run away from difficult or frightening situations in my life?**
- **Do I put on a facade that everything is perfect when, in fact, I am hurting inside and need support from loved ones?**
- **Do I provide comfort to family members or friends who are suffering?**

Intercessory prayer

Ask, and it will be given you; search, and you will find; knock, and the door will be opened for you. For everyone who asks receives, and everyone who searches finds, and for everyone who knocks, the door will be opened. (Luke 11.9-10)

Let us not downplay prayer of petition, which so often calms our hearts and helps us persevere in hope. Prayer of intercession has particular value, for it is an act of trust in God and, at the same time, an expression of love for our neighbour. (*Gaudete et Exsultate*, 154)

- **Do I pray with perseverance for the needs of others to be met?**
- **Do I trust that God will answer those prayers, sometimes in ways beyond my understanding?**
- **Do I see my own personal prayer as contributing to the life of society and the Christian community?**

The strong man

No one can enter a strong man's house and plunder his property without first tying up the strong man. (Mark 3.27)

The Christian life is a constant battle. We need strength and courage to withstand the temptations of the devil and to proclaim the Gospel. This battle is sweet, for it allows us to rejoice each time the Lord triumphs in our lives. (*Gaudete et Exsultate*, 158)

- **Do I believe the devil is actively trying to lead me away from God?**
- **Do I pray for and try to develop the gift of being able to discern which impulses come from God and which from the devil?**
- **Do I avoid situations where I might be more susceptible to temptations?**

MY ROLE IN THE FAMILY

The present moment

Live in love, as Christ loved us and gave himself up for us, a fragrant offering and sacrifice to God. (Ephesians 5.2)

In many cases, parents come home exhausted, not wanting to talk, and many families no longer even share a common meal. Distractions abound, including an addiction to television. This makes it all the more difficult for parents to hand on the faith to their children ... [Families] often seem more caught up with securing their future than with enjoying the present. (*Amoris Laetitia,* 50)

- **Do I give enough of my time and energy to my spouse and our children?**
- **Do I put aside the inevitable distractions from outside the home to give quality time to my family?**
- **Am I passing on the faith to our children?**

Living with Christ 11

Family dialogue

Be angry but do not sin; do not let the sun go down on your anger. (Ephesians 4.26)

As the Bishops of Mexico have pointed out, violence within families breeds new forms of social aggression, since "family relationships can also explain the tendency to a violent personality. [...] Violence within the family is a breeding-ground of resentment and hatred in the most basic human relationships." (*Amoris Laetitia,* 51)

- **Do I encourage open, non-threatening dialogue among my family members?**
- **Do I use physical force in trying to overcome disagreements?**
- **Do I verbally abuse members of my family?**

Equal dignity

Be subject to one another out of reverence for Christ. (Ephesians 5.21)

History is burdened by the excesses of patriarchal cultures that considered women inferior, yet in our own day, we cannot overlook the use of surrogate mothers and "the exploitation and commercialization of the female body in the current media culture." [...] The equal dignity of men and women makes us rejoice to see old forms of discrimination disappear, and within families there is a growing reciprocity. (*Amoris Laetitia*, 54)

- **Do I respect the equal dignity of women and men at home, in the workplace and throughout society?**
- **Do I do my share of the work in maintaining the household?**
- **Do I love my spouse with the same dedication with which Christ loved the Church?**
- **Do I tell jokes that are racist or sexist, or remain silent when other people do?**

An imperfect world

Love is patient. (1 Corinthians 13.4)

Being patient does not mean letting ourselves be constantly mistreated, tolerating physical aggression or allowing other people to use us. We encounter problems whenever we think that relationships or people ought to be perfect, or when we put ourselves at the centre and expect things to turn out our way. Then everything makes us impatient, everything makes us react aggressively. Unless we cultivate patience, we will always find excuses for responding angrily. (*Amoris Laetitia,* 92)

- **Do I accept people just as they are in this world, with all their idiosyncrasies?**
- **Do I respectfully speak out when I or others are abused or treated unjustly?**
- **How do I understand time – as my personal possession or as a means to be of service to God and others?**

Children's development

Let the little children come to me, and do not stop them; for it is to such as these that the kingdom of God belongs. (Luke 18.16)

Parents always influence the moral development of their children, for better or for worse. It follows that they should take up this essential role and carry it out consciously, enthusiastically, reasonably and appropriately. (*Amoris Laetitia*, 259)

- **Do I welcome children into our family?**
- **Do I strive to form them in Christian values by showing respect for their dignity, their freedom and their need for discipline?**
- **Do I model the virtues children should emulate?**

Family prayer

I bow my knees before the Father, from whom every family in heaven and on earth takes its name. (Ephesians 3.14-15)

If a family is centred on Christ, he will unify and illumine its entire life. Moments of pain and difficulty will be experienced in union with the Lord's cross, and his closeness will make it possible to surmount them. In the darkest hours of a family's life, union with Jesus in his abandonment can help avoid a breakup. (*Amoris Laetitia,* 317)

- **Do I see the family as a place where all its members can grow in holiness?**
- **Is family prayer a regular part of my family's culture?**
- **Do I rely on Christ to help turn our dark times into an offering of love?**

Dignity of the elderly

Do not cast me off in the time of old age; do not forsake me when my strength is spent. (Psalm 71.9)

In highly industrialized societies, where the number of elderly persons is growing even as the birth rate declines, they can be regarded as a burden. On the other hand, the care that they require often puts a strain on their loved ones. Care and concern for the final stages of life is all the more necessary today, when contemporary society attempts to remove every trace of death and dying. (*Amoris Laetitia,* 48)

- **Do I respect the dignity of elderly people, especially those who have physical disabilities or dementia?**

- **Do I see assisted suicide as an acceptable option for myself or for those close to me?**

- **Do I reach out to those who are lonely or isolated?**

DISEASES OF THE WORKPLACE

Lords and masters

All who exalt themselves will be humbled, and all who humble themselves will be exalted. (Matthew 23.12)

The disease of thinking we are "immortal," "immune" or downright "indispensable," neglecting the need for regular check-ups… It is the disease of the rich fool in the Gospel, who thought he would live forever (cf. Luke 12.13-21), but also of those who turn into lords and masters, and think of themselves as above others and not at their service. (*Pope Francis' 2014 Christmas Greetings to the Roman Curia*)

- **Do I see myself as part of a team or as superior to my co-workers?**
- **Do I focus on service to others or do I avoid sharing my talents?**
- **What legacy do I want to leave for future generations?**

Work addictions

Martha, Martha, you are worried and distracted by many things; there is need of only one thing. (Luke 10.41-42)

Another disease is the "Martha complex," excessive busy-ness. It is found in those who immerse themselves in work and inevitably neglect "the better part": sitting at the feet of Jesus (cf. Luke 10.38-42)… A time of rest, for those who have completed their work, is necessary, obligatory and should be taken seriously: by spending time with one's family and respecting holidays as moments of spiritual and physical recharging. *(Pope Francis' 2014 Christmas Greetings to the Roman Curia)*

- **Am I addicted to my work?**
- **Do I believe that my own efforts are more effective than the ways in which God acts through me?**
- **Do I act as though work is more important than sharing myself and my time with family and friends?**

Excessive planning

The wind blows where it chooses, and you hear the sound of it, but you do not know where it comes from or where it goes. So it is with everyone who is born of the Spirit. (John 3.8)

When the apostle plans everything down to the last detail and believes that with perfect planning things will fall into place, he becomes an accountant or an office manager. Things need to be prepared well, but without ever falling into the temptation of trying to contain and direct the freedom of the Holy Spirit, which is always greater and more flexible than any human planning. (*Pope Francis' 2014 Christmas Greetings to the Roman Curia*)

- **Do I replace mercy and spontaneity with excessive policy making and planning?**
- **Do I act as though human order is more important than openness to the Holy Spirit?**
- **Do I listen for the Holy Spirit speaking through the voices of others?**

Sowers of weeds

A gossip goes about telling secrets, but one who is trustworthy in spirit keeps a confidence. (Proverbs 11.13)

The disease of gossiping, grumbling and back-biting… It is a grave illness which begins simply, perhaps even in small talk, and takes over a person, making him become a "sower of weeds" (like Satan) and in many cases, a cold-blooded killer of the good name of our colleagues… It is the disease of cowardly persons who lack the courage to speak out directly, but instead speak behind other people's backs. (*Pope Francis' 2014 Christmas Greetings to the Roman Curia*)

- **Am I eager for bad news about others to tickle my ears?**
- **At work and at home, do I focus on what others are doing wrong rather than on what I could be doing right or better?**
- **Do I use words to harm others' reputations?**

The workplace ladder

Those who belong to Christ Jesus have crucified the flesh with its passions and desires... Let us not become conceited, competing against one another, envying one another. (Galatians 5.24, 26)

The disease of idolizing superiors. This is the disease of those who court their superiors in the hope of gaining their favour. They are victims of careerism and opportunism; they honour persons and not God (cf. Matthew 23.8-12). They serve thinking only of what they can get and not of what they should give. Superiors themselves could be affected by this disease, when they court their collaborators in order to obtain their submission, loyalty and psychological dependency. (*Pope Francis' 2014 Christmas Greetings to the Roman Curia*)

- **Is climbing the corporate ladder or obtaining advantages for myself the chief goal of my work?**

- **Do I have an ongoing competition with a co-worker?**

- **Do I resent being passed over for a promotion?**

A closed circle

Every kingdom divided against itself becomes a desert, and house falls on house. (Luke 11.17)

The disease of closed circles, where belonging to a clique becomes more powerful than belonging to the Body and, in some circumstances, to Christ himself. This disease too always begins with good intentions, but with the passing of time it enslaves its members and becomes a cancer which threatens the harmony of the Body. (*Pope Francis' 2014 Christmas Greetings to the Roman Curia*)

- **Do I nurture the life of an in-group which excludes others?**

- **Do I open the circle by drawing newcomers and those of a different race or faith into the fold?**

- **Do I act out of the belief that my neighbour includes everybody?**

MY CONTRIBUTION TO SOCIETY

The simple life

Be on your guard against all kinds of greed; for one's life does not consist in the abundance of possessions. (Luke 12.15)

Since the market tends to promote extreme consumerism in an effort to sell its products, people can easily get caught up in a whirlwind of needless buying and spending. Compulsive consumerism is one example of how the techno-economic paradigm affects individuals… The emptier a person's heart is, the more he or she needs things to buy, own and consume. It becomes almost impossible to accept the limits imposed by reality. (*Laudato Si'*, 203–204)

- **Do I engage in excessive travel or use a vehicle which consumes an inordinate amount of the earth's resources?**
- **Am I addicted to purchasing?**
- **What concrete actions do I take to protect the environment?**
- **Do I share the fruits of my labour with those who have less?**

Indifference in the face of suffering

Truly I tell you, just as you did it to one of the least of these who are members of my family, you did it to me. (Matthew 25.40)

The *social character* of mercy demands that we not simply stand by and do nothing. It requires us to banish indifference and hypocrisy, lest our plans and projects remain a dead letter. [...] We are called to promote a *culture of mercy* based on the rediscovery of encounter with others, a culture in which no one looks at another with indifference or turns away from the suffering of our brothers and sisters. (*Misericordia et Misera*, 19–20)

- **Do I participate in at least one of the works of mercy?**
- **How am I working to change the unjust structures of society?**
- **Do I see Jesus in the faces of those who are in need?**

The marginalized

If one member suffers, all suffer together with it; if one member is honoured, all rejoice together with it. (1 Corinthians 12.26)

The poor hear voices scolding them, telling them to be quiet and to put up with their lot. These voices are harsh, often due to fear of the poor, who are considered not only destitute but also a source of insecurity and unrest, an unwelcome distraction from life as usual and needing to be rejected and kept afar.
(*Message for the 2017 World Day of the Poor*, 5)

- **Do I reject those who are marginalized through poverty, race, sexual orientation or religious beliefs?**

- **Do I reach out to those who are marginalized and welcome them into mainstream society?**

- **Do I support political actions which worsen the plight of the marginalized?**

Historical divisions

The Samaritan woman said to him, "How is it that you, a Jew, ask a drink of me, a woman of Samaria?" (John 4.9)

Those wounded by historical divisions find it difficult to accept our invitation to forgiveness and reconciliation, since they think that we are ignoring their pain or are asking them to give up their memory and ideals. But if they see the witness of authentically fraternal and reconciled communities, they will find that witness luminous and attractive. (*Gaudete et Exsultate,* 100)

- Do I respect the traditions and beliefs of people of faiths, cultures and ethnicities that are different from mine?
- Do I expect them to conform to my point of view or do I enter into a dialogue which seeks mutual understanding?
- Do I attempt to spread the Gospel by winning arguments more than by winning friends?

Fake news

You will know the truth, and the truth will make you free. (John 8.32)

There is no such thing as harmless disinformation; on the contrary, trusting in falsehood can have dire consequences. Even a seemingly slight distortion of the truth can have dangerous effects. (*Message for 2018 World Communications Day,* 3)

- **Does the news I read and share with others come from reputable sources?**
- **Do I allow deceptive language and falsehoods to darken my inner life?**
- **Am I skeptical of news sources which strive to increase the power of some ideology?**

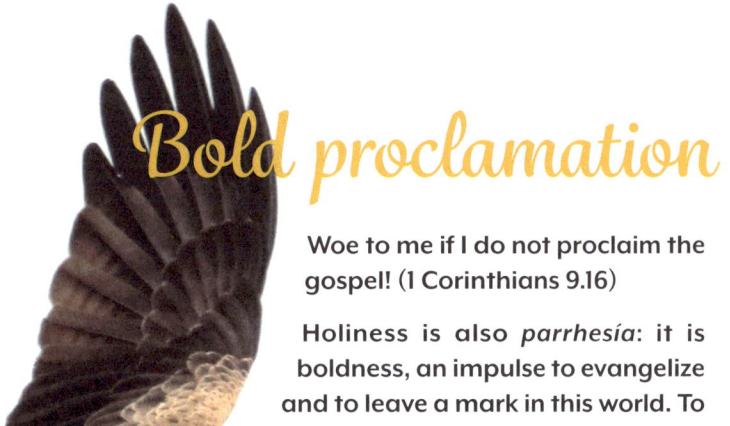

Bold proclamation

Woe to me if I do not proclaim the gospel! (1 Corinthians 9.16)

Holiness is also *parrhesía*: it is boldness, an impulse to evangelize and to leave a mark in this world. To allow us to do this, Jesus himself comes and tells us once more, serenely yet firmly: "Do not be afraid" (Mark 6.50). (*Gaudete et Exsultate,* 129)

- **Do I fail to proclaim God's word or the Church's social teaching because I fear a negative reaction?**

- **Am I weak in my belief that God is always with his followers?**

- **Am I afraid to stand out from the crowd?**

From words to action

Let justice roll down like waters, and righteousness like an ever-flowing stream. (Amos 5.24)

Complacency is seductive; it tells us that there is no point in trying to change things, that there is nothing we can do, because this is the way things have always been and yet we always manage to survive. By force of habit we no longer stand up to evil. We "let things be," or as others have decided they ought to be. (*Gaudete et Exsultate*, 137)

- **How am I complicit in environmental devastation and social injustice?**
- **Do I take responsibility for changing the societal structures which give rise to such evils?**
- **Do I accept things as they are without examining how I could make them better?**

Conclusion

Create in me a clean heart, O God, and put a new and right spirit within me. (Psalm 51.10)

Human beings, while capable of the worst, are also capable of rising above themselves, choosing again what is good, and making a new start, despite their mental and social conditioning. We are able to take an honest look at ourselves, to acknowledge our deep dissatisfaction, and to embark on new paths to authentic freedom. No system can completely suppress our openness to what is good, true and beautiful, or our God-given ability to respond to his grace at work deep in our hearts. (*Laudato Si'*, 205)

- **Do I blame society or other people for the wrongs that I do?**
- **Do I have a plan for making a new start by "rising above myself" and choosing what is good?**
- **How can I achieve true freedom?**

SPECIAL ISSUE: Living with Christ

**Published in the United States by
Bayard, Inc.**
Publisher: Joseph Sinasac
Associate Publisher: Richard Lamoureux, AA
Editor: Janina Shook Silvestri
janina.silvestri@bayard-inc.com

Business Office:
Bayard, Inc.
One Montauk Ave, Suite 200
New London, CT 06320
tel: 1-800-321-0411
www.livingwithchrist.us
ISBN: 978-1-62785-480-1
Date of Issue: August 2019

Published in Canada by Novalis
Publisher: Joseph Sinasac
Editor: Natalia Kononenko
LWC@novalis.ca
Associate Editor: Nancy Keyes
Layout and Design: Jessica Llewellyn

Business Office:
Novalis, Periodicals Dept.
1 Eglinton Avenue East, Suite 800
Toronto, ON M4P 3A1
tel: (416) 363-3303
fax: (416) 363-9409
email: living@novalis.ca
www.livingwithchrist.ca
ISBN: 978-2-89688-722-4
Date of Issue: August 2019

Printed in Canada.

All rights reserved. No part of this publication may be reproduced, stored in a retrieval system, or transmitted in any form, or by any means, electronic, mechanical, photocopying, recording, or otherwise, without the written permission of the publisher.

All Pope Francis texts referenced in this publication are ©Libreria Editrice Vaticana, 2019.

Photos: Dreamstime.com: pp. 25-31; Shutterstock.com: cover, p. 1, pp. 3-24.